LETTERS OF THE PRIESTESS

VERSES TO IGNITE INNER EVOLUTION

PAULA T. CURTEANU

I don't wish to be a Queen, nor an Empress.
I only need to reside in the Kingdom of my Soul.
I am therefore the Highest Priestess.

This book is dedicated to all those
who have a devotion to inner life,
a love of understanding themselves and others
so that we can all live in a kinder world
and create a place free of division,
where who we become
is more important than what we say
and even than what we do.
A place where we would want our children to grow:
a compassionate world.
To you, all Priestesses and Priests of the highest order, that is:
loving who we are.

To my son, the one and only Benito

Letters Of The Priestess by Paula T. Curteanu
1st Edition Paperback 2nd February 2022

First published in the United Kingdom 2022 by Paula T. Curteanu

Book cover & design: Paula T. Curteanu
Illustrations: Paula T. Curteanu
Editor: Denise Wakeling
Typesetting InDesign: Hari Dharmendra

ISBN: 978-1-7398919-0-9

Printed by Lightning Source 2021 - 2022

CONTENTS

Part II
Of the Inner World

Part III
Of the Other World

Epilogue

Prologue

I have a vision where even if I achieve nothing more in this life, even if no one will read my book, even if I never travel anywhere or meet anyone new or never be in love again, or never be able to move again, I realise with every cell in my body that I am enough, as I am now, that my presence here in this world is an incredible miracle in itself, a gift to me and anyone who knows me and doesn't know me, or anyone who will simply eat the food from the ground my feet walked on. You may say I am fertiliser, but I say I am Life. Maybe then, when I grasp it, what I do and who I am will finally become One.
One with Life itself.

~

This book was a long time coming for me. I was one year old when an audience first witnessed my writing. Back home we celebrate this milestone with a ritual called 'Ruperea Turtei'. The closest translation I can offer would be 'break off the sweet bread'. Someone had baked a sweet bread, placed it above my head and broke off pieces for all the family to eat (for abundance). I was vigorously lifted up, all the way to the ceiling, three times for good luck. Finally, several items of interest were laid out on a silver tray for me to 'choose'- house keys, money, a pen, a hair brush. Whatever I decided to take from the tray, would be a sign of my future calling.

I picked up the pen and I got right into it: making my own marks in a language only I could speak, recorded on anything I could find - my hand, someone's face, the ground. I favourited writing on the wall and I still do. Except now they make magnetic paper. What a magical invention!

Through the eyes of a one-year-old, writing was just that: a joyful experience. As I grew up things changed. Other values became more important than me expressing myself: school achievements, family, being a good daughter, then being a good mother and the list goes on. There was an unlimited source of limiting excuses - coming from a communist country, with a violent past and culture and overall disrupted life dynamic.

The further east you travel, the more women become less worthy of dignity. Add a touch of personal strife - moving home and relocating in three countries, divorce, financial pressure, life-threatening conditions, more heart break. You name it. There is nothing from the list of trauma inducing events known to humans, which I have not at least witnessed closely, if not directly experienced. But it is not about who did what, when and to whom. This work is about *who I choose to become.*

All the reasons I mentioned could have easily remained a very long list of excuses and illusions maintained only by the dichotomy of the world we find ourselves in. A patriarchal world where achievement is perceived and measured in material ways. Where what we do to obtain achievements (whatever achievement means), is more valued than who we are willing to become.

However, there is nothing more important than who we become. Only I can truly know who I have become.

Who I choose to be, in order to live this one life in integrity, truth and love must be my holy ground, my religion and my faith. The non-negotiable inborn 'I AM' must remain, no matter what boxes we think we need to tick in order to get love and approval from others.

Like many women of our days, I had to work, live, move like a man to break even. Lacking a consistent, positive example of what masculinity meant, I had internalised patriarchy in such a distorted way, even my inner contemplation was soldier-like. Wake up early, workout, meditate, push and push through. For results. A result oriented life.

But what I had managed to push was my feminine side - it was so far away, I couldn't remember how to be alone. Please know this is nothing to do with gender. No matter what gender we identify as, we have 'a Do and a Be' side. The left and the right brain. IQ and EQ. That's the masculine and feminine I am speaking about. Although men seem to have benefited from patriarchy, it is merely a golden cage. So many men have lost their soul trying to be who their ancestors taught them to be, in the name of safety and survival.

Too many of us, whether a she/her, he/him or they/them, we all overtly or secretly diminish and banish our feminine fundamentals. "Don't cry like a girl", "Don't be such a *ussy" are some of the well-known ones. Sadly the list of pejoratives addressed to feminine expression in this world are too many to list. The most inspiring men I ever met have no issue crying. And the most inspiring women I ever met, have no issue wiping their tears when it's time.

As I found myself turning deeper inwards, in the moments

of stillness I would steal as often as possible, I could only see images of a Priestess. At least that's what my mind made of it. I would sip my coffee in the morning (I take at least ten minutes alone with a coffee before I speak to anyone everyday) and there she would be. A gentle yet fierce monastic presence, who makes daily introspection a priority in her life. Something ancient, a part of me, and each of us, that had always been there, but was becoming dimmer and dimmer in this loud, rushed world. The discipline alone (the positive masculine ingredient) wasn't enough for my inner exploration.

I didn't really know what was missing. I had to learn along the way: it turned out to be *devotion.* Devotion is love in action. Consistent care and attention towards something of value. It was the Priestess imagery and wisdom archetype that helped me join the dots. Through writing. Writing was always my most faithful friend. It offered a grounded stillness, a peaceful strength and an intuitive movement of the pen on paper. Which is what a writer is after all, a channel of creative power. When we create anything, we are in the feminine. When we give it a supportive container, that's the masculine. We need both in the world, now more than ever.

A myriad of synchronicities took place once I committed to writing. In the Acknowledgements section I am detailing the connection with a Sumerian High Priestess who showed up along the way to inspire me. But do leave that part at the end, so you can first read the story like I wrote it: innocent of any facts and data.

And so I ended up piecing this book together, with no research on archetypes or history. On purpose. I just wanted to see what comes up.

At first I wrote short introspective essays, as that's what I always did. Then my prose turned more lyrical. And as many of us have experienced, the pandemic squeezed the poetry out of us. When my inquiry reached an end (what I named the Letters), some other type of language formed. We can call it Poetry or it's maybe just a different language from another side of our minds. And then when I ran out of words, I drew. And finally I could just be still.

Then I made a book cover and learned how to publish. All writers dream of being published with a big name. There is nothing wrong in that when you wish your message to reach others. But if you put the value of your writing in the size of your audience, you have misunderstood writing as expression, as a gift. It was Maya Angelou who said: "There is no greater agony than bearing an untold story inside you." It was when I wrote 'The End' that I knew what she meant, and what being a writer really is. All I can say is: publishing is overrated. I started writing a book and it finished with the book re-writing me.

I pray this collection of words and images finds you right where you need it the most, in the same way some books I love found me when I needed them. Everything I have written here is self-addressed, lived and experienced. And although there is nothing new in the world, it may offer you the comfort that you are not alone.

With great love and devotion,

Your Priestess.

PART I

OF THE OUTER WORLD

THE NIGHT WHEN THE MOON WAS FULL OF SILVER

One night when the Moon was full of silver, the Priestess broke the rules of the covenant. She raised her voice in holy anger against a High Priest who wore the ego dressed in God's clothing. Devotion was her path, richness was his. He conjured up empty words of promise and collected money from believers. She knew his heart had been closed and he was making coins of the mind to buy him righteousness. He refused to hear her, and he had her imprisoned by dawn. Guards locked her cell, she was named a Luna-tic.

~

The Priestess carries pen and paper under her robes. She can see the light of the moon through the window at the end of a narrow dark corridor leading to her confinement. The tide is high, washing the stone walls of the tower she is locked in. She will write at night when the guard is asleep. And maybe, just maybe, the world will hear her voice once more.

LETTER 1

Freedom, not what you seek but what seeks you.

Beloved

I seek you, knowingly and unknowingly, but what are you?
Pray I see you clearly tonight. The guard will be asleep,
the moon is half.

I have thirsted and hungered so long in a world where I am
only who the Man sees. Why do I seek approval when the
Man seeks enlightenment? And why is my Master teacher
wearing the robe made by the hands of a woman?

I spoke too much, my tongue got me exiled.
In silence I find my island.

FREEDOM

Like heat rising from the concrete pavement
Like silence rising from the heart of night
Like sunrise kissing the forehead of horizon
That's how freedom rises in you.

Like earth hugging roots of trees unseen
Like oceans holding land together
Like mountains holding up the sky
that's how freedom's holding you.

You know all there is to know
You lived how they said you should
You made all your dreams come true
Still, you've not touched freedom.

You played chess with your mind and won
You counted beads of your sins with your fingertips
You redeemed all your shortcomings in full
Yet, you've not tasted freedom.

Undress yourself of old rags
Ride the horse of innocence on the beach of life
Maybe then you will
Set freedom free.

LETTER 2

Beloved

My heart breaks for all believers. Those who make their beliefs so tough like rock, as it's the only way that the world feels safe and of comfort. For they will miss the fluidity of life itself. The wonder of navigating the ordinary and the miracles alike.

When I blindly believe, as good as that belief may seem, I become rigid and disconnected from my closest ones. That's when I feel at my loneliest.

My heart breaks for all souls who realise it, but fear they are so deeply ingrained, they stop trying.

For all of us my heart weeps and all of you I love the same. So I pray.

PRAYER

I pray for you:

I pray that you see the unseen
You hear the unspoken
You tell the untold
You sing the unsung
You feel the unfelt
You dream the unimaginable.

That you climb the highest mountain
You dive in the deepest sea
You smell the scent of freedom
You taste the flesh of life.

I pray for you:

That the angels take your pain
The rain washes your sins
The sun dries your wounds
The night rests your mind
The wind picks up your soul,
Takes it to the place
Where the eye that showed you God
Is the same eye as God's eye
And with the eye
That I see you
When I don't see you

I pray:

LETTER 3

Beloved

What is home to you?
Your origin?
Your destination?
Somewhere you come from or somewhere you arrive?
A place or a person?

I see now that my home never leaves me, no matter where I am.
This place where only I can live.

Travel safe.

HOME

What is home, but where your soul breathes lighter

The soil from the place where you're born
Travels inside your bones
And feeds your marrow
But only to grow wings at the ends
So you can fly wherever

The rain from the clouds where you're born
washed your skin
Only to prepare it to be drenched by the sun
That shines the same light
Everywhere

And those dearest to you from the land you're born
Like the wind, they fill your sails
Taking your boat to places
Otherwise unknown

My home, I've never missed you
Because you're with me
Everywhere
I go.

LETTER 4

Beloved

I have reached the end of all the reasons why it shouldn't be me. All the excuses I make, just make it about me.

But it isn't about me. How arrogant to think the world is about me.

Only I am about the world. From the world. And in the world I host my voice and this body.

None of it is mine.

EXPRESSION

Say what you're here to say
Paint the sky with the brush stroke of your eye
Sing the melody of your heart
To the ear of our souls
Draw lines that turn into foundations
That turn into buildings
That host our bodies
Warm our flesh
Make numbers turn love into action
Dreams into reality
Grief into hope

Create a day that always ends with
I love you, may that be just to yourself

Sleep knowing there are more tomorrows
To your days
But don't wait until you run out of tomorrows
As there is nothing more selfish
Than hiding a gift offered
From the world that feeds you
Gifts in every moment
Puts the paintbrush in your hand
And the song in your voice
Just open your mouth
Move your hand
And be alive.

LETTER 5

Beloved

There is a split in all of us as old as the sun and the shadow it creates on earth. As ancient as the flux and reflux of the sea and as vital as the inhale and exhale.

But which one of us has ever only taken air out and not in, and lived?

Those we judge for wrongs, are they never right?
Those who believe to be righteous, passively overlook wrongdoing, when it's not their house being broken.

When you see someone hungry, do you offer them a meal or let them die? Then shout in anger at thieves who become murderers to survive.

Either we are all guilty, or we are all innocent.
All believers are innocent of their beliefs.

Right and Wrong

Tired of battles fought in vain
Blood lost, river running red
While judges and jurors,
Criminals and victims
Wearing clothes made of the same thread
In the same world, under the same sun

Blind leading the blind
Whilst the ones with the gift of sight
are busy making more thread.

Does the bird song remind you
How to turn rivalry into melody?
Hear the changing of the season
Whispering to rest in reason
but to move in passion?

Don't move in guilt and shame
Don't point fingers to blame

As all fingers belong to the same hand
When one finger breaks, the whole hand suffers
and the other fingers don't punish each other,
instead they work together
to still have a hand.

LETTER 6

Family, not a cult, but an embrace.

Beloved

When you left the world behind, your mother, your father, your sister, your brother, did you not find them again, as soon as you arrived here?

Can you ever leave them, and can they ever leave you? For your veins carry them from then until now and evermore.

And when you arrived and met your new family, the soul one, and you grew kinder, did you ask the world, what is family?

What is the world, but your family away from home.

FAMILY

Shelter from the rain outside
A strangers smile when it's lonely inside
Friends laughter at the end of a long day
Or little paws that make everything ok
Any of these are family to me
But when bound by law and blood
We look at each other in mirrors
Searching our reflection in another
Yet, our heads are too high
Or the arms are too long
Or the mirror too narrow?
Nay, we shall love and behold
And the things we do for beholding:
Feed the belly, starve the soul
Smile with teeth, cry with blood
Make love in the dark, wake up unloved
Protect the home, to hell with others
But donate at church on Sunday.
And kill if we must save our children
From life itself

Close your eyes, to hold on
On to us, or onto them
Onto beliefs long forgone
Renouncing our tomorrow
For the Family.
In the name of love.

LETTER 7

Beloved

If I were the best mother and you were the best father, our children would never be ours. They would only belong to freedom. We would nurture them into being kings and queens of their own souls and we would never make their lives our trophies.

If we lived our lives through theirs, we would occupy a space that's not ours.

We must return what we borrow.

CHILDREN

Your eyes, my lips
The soul, their own.

Your hands, my smile
The life they choose.

Breath from heaven
Body from earth
The heart, only they can open.

Protect them from the brunt of your fears
Ease them of the load of your convictions
Teach them to clean the plates of expectations.

Father, take off the veil of bloodline
so you can see the light in their eye
Mother, remove the limits of the sky
for there is no sky, only stars
Gift them the gold of freedom
The diamonds of love
The castles of wisdom.

Our children are not our children
Rain is not our rain
Wind is not our wind
The life you borrowed,
Return it
To our children

LETTER 8

Beloved

I had a dream about marriage. I was told about it in my reality, but I didn't quite understand it. So I was shown in my sleep.

There are three kinds of marriages.
The marriage with another here on earth.
The marriage with another up above.
And the marriage with oneself, on earth and above.

No one can be married to another fully but not be married to oneself.
Each one of the three is fragile, but only the last one can outlast the others.
People have been together and then not together from the beginning until the end of time.

Yet there is something sacred in union with oneself, that brings union with all there is around.
And that may include another.

Marriage

There are two cedar trees at the end of my garden
Each leaning onto each other
But each standing tall on its own

So tall their crowns talk to heaven
The trunks bearing signs of suns and storms
Each rooted deeply underground
Nurtured by hundreds of layers of snow and ice

Their branches joined together at the top
Only after each one grew enough bark
To bear the brunt of life
One takes the northerly winds
The other the southern sun

They could each stand alone and be just fine
And so they did at first
But as they grew, their branches reached each other
Like fingers intertwined
Then arms around each other
Standing side by side
Walking the path of seasons
Until their crowns turned into one
Like a temple of life
Built by two cedar trees
That didn't need each other
But found each other either way.

LETTER 9

"It only takes one to love", Byron Katie

Beloved

Nothing lasts forever except love.
In life on earth school, sometimes I separate from others, from places and even from myself.
But it doesn't mean I have to separate from love.
Only then, I suffer.
If I let the love exist and I don't try to erase it, I just lovingly part from anything and anyone.
I can divorce with love, but not from it.
Sometimes I loved reality, other times I loved imagination.

Either way, I loved and nothing can change that.

DIVORCE

I dreamt of mornings drenched in sun
Of travels on clear waters
Fields of gold engulfing us
Dances lit by winter flames

And I woke up with the sound of rain
Closed roads flooded with tears of many
Dried lands excavated in hunts for gold
Damp coals in placid ashes left to mold

No one's to blame for my dreams, nor my reality
I try to reminisce my way to sobriety
And as the sunset wind whispers untold stories
In unfinished symphonies of sunrise glory

I turn my head slightly to the left
Lean over gently on the edge adrift
To hear that sound, like someone's near
What is it, can you tell my dear

Lub dub lub dub
reverberating rhythm of life
pumping blood in percussive beats
love lost
love found
love be

LETTER 10

"For in the the dew of little things the heart finds its morning and it's refreshed." K. Gibran

Beloved

As I sat here alone thinking about friendship, I can only think of one true best friend. One who was with me since birth and even before then. One who wakes up with me and goes to bed with me everyday, even when I don't fully approve or like them. This one friend has never left my side. And when I realise that, I stop expecting others to fill in this role. Now others just show up as themselves. What a joy, to just be a friend.

And then I think of other friends who have come and gone, some with time, some with false pretences. Never keep friendships in disguise. Those that remain, only have one thing in common - a kinder world. A deeper life.

There is no place where life is deeper than when you laugh with a friend, knowing you can be just yourself.
Your best friend.

FRIENDSHIP

Blades of grass
All swing together
That way or this way
The wind tells them where to look
Until their eyes get dry
And tired they lay still in the sunset
Resting their little chlorophyl legs

Thirsty
No one told them they have water inside,

So a friend comes in, the night
With no pointing fingers
Just cold honest hands
The dark catches water
Making magic with no audience
With cool embraces
Turning vapour into love
Dripping quietly
On gentle green sleepy blades of grass

When the first light of day
Touches their face
They wake up covered in diamonds
They always had but didn't know

What a precious friend the night is.

LETTER 11

Beloved

No one needs saving. No one is beneath anyone.

The best teachers are not here to teach, they are here to live from deeper places. Places we see mirrored in us, places that draw us in, to familiar sites.

The best teachers don't teach.
They are friends who we meet on a walk.

TEACHING

Teacher
how far would you walk for your teaching?
What bridges would you cross?
Journeys with no scenic views
Full of crossroads in curious towns

You travel neither light nor heavy
You carry your belongings with dignity
Shining a light along the way

Lighting up paths not just for you
But for all those walking that way
Beside you, or around you

Because light always reaches farther than its source

You walk your path, lighting away
And they may join you, either way
You walk

And you don't quite know why
You could try to say it
but words wouldn't quite capture it.

Together we walk.

LETTER 12

Beloved

The gift of the tongues belongs to everyone. Those who decide they will open their mouths and allow the words to come through them are blessed. Words come and go and you can't hold on to them, try to remember them, scribe them into rock.

How many ways can we speak in?

SPEAKING

Speaker
Holy words come out of your unholy flesh
Who cares who said it
If it travels to the right ears
Enters the blood stream
Reaches the heart
Then you are done

Speaker of holy revenge
Drive divine anger into the cracks of this world and either
Bring it together or tear it apart to be rebuild again
Maybe a better human race will rise
Who are you to know otherwise

Speaker
Take a deep breath in
Bring life onto unsaid things
Speaker
Stand up and speak for those who have no voice
It was taken away from them
by those asleep in this world
Speaker
When there will be nothing left in the world
There will only be the Word
And then just Silence
And from there you are born.
Speaker of life

LETTER 13

Beloved

What is learning? Repeating words by heart? A sum of knowledge, or a loss of it?

Or is it maybe becoming undefended to receive lessons, by actually practicing instead of theorising.

When a parent supports a child with their first steps, it is so they can learn to run free, with no support.

There is no book for that.

LEARNING

First baby steps
Wobbly shapes of courage
You are born with the fear of falling
But the desire to move overcomes it
Risking to tumble
You step ahead regardless

One foot on the ground another in the air
Hold on to something
But best grip nothing
That way you can make your footsteps
Traces you can follow again and again
Reminding you when you used to crawl

Doing it, the best teacher of all.

LETTER 14

Choice, the most divine part of the human experience.

Beloved

I went to the bottom of the ocean and up on Cloud 9 with ease, yet I couldn't easily choose you.

I struggled in guilt, shame and regret until I lost sight of myself, you and the world.

There is nothing more tragic than choosing to abdicate the power of choice. No one is shackled. Even when there's a weapon pushing against your flesh, you still have a choice.

You can still face your weapon with dignity and not lose a moment of being alive. Not one.

Don't be so arrogant as to think you know what's better for others. In doing so, you take away the chance life gives them to make their own choices. That is unkind. It belongs to the Ego, not to Love.

Either sleep or awake.

CHOICE

When you wait too long to choose,
You're selfish.
When you're rushing,
you're foolish.

Yet it is better to make a choice sooner,
Don't let it turn into a tumour.
Then if life doesn't consent,
You can listen, make amends
Trust life to apprehend.

But making no choice, everyone looses
Time goes by, self hate induces
Luxury of choice rolls over
And necessity takes over.
Choice-less, you passover.

If your choice is just for others
Your heart's song drowned in violence
You're a fraud, not a saint
You trade yourself up to get love in return
A poisoned chalice, your soul will burn.

If your choice is just for you,
Twisting self-love into concepts askew
Compassion gone from your life's preview
You're just a coward
By ego's mouth of fear devoured.

Only the truth is always the right choice
A lie with an elaborate excuse, only the coward's ploys.
The truth is only for the brave
Yet choose truth always,

Go on, leave your cave.

PART II

OF THE INNER WORLD

The Tide Is High, The Moon Not Full

The Priestess has been praying and writing in the moonlight. The Moon has seen the Priestess's face and has taken the tide higher than before, on the new moon. The tide flooded the Guard's quarters.

The Guard fears water rising, so he moves the Priestess in the cell higher up, where water doesn't reach. He opens three gates and the Priestess gets dry clean clothes.

The Guard glances at her writing. She lets him read, if he brings her a candle to write longer at night.

LETTER 15

Pain, not something to avoid, but a trusted medicine for poisoned thoughts.

Beloved

You took a long time to see, but now your eyes are open. It hurts more to keep thoughts trapped inside cages, than embracing them with curiosity.
The birds don't sing here, the air is too rare. The guard will leave at twilight.

Time is yours.

PAIN

Your eyes pulsate with the beat of your heart
Your heart burns in the heat of your anger
Your anger drowns in the sorrow of your soul
Your soul trapped by the chains of your thoughts
Your thoughts cemented in the fears of your father
Your father innocent of your beliefs

But round and' round the pain you go.
Story retold, meaning forgotten.

The wave once formed won't be broken until land
The fire once lit won't die out until dawn
The walls of your heart will grow taller at night
Let it wash over you.
Welcome its piercing embrace
Cherish its bitter medicine
Rejoice in the iced water
With your missing limbs
Swim through the swamp of the misunderstood
Washup on the shore of innocence
And when the sun dries out the dirt in your hair
And the salt on your skin
You will open your mouth
And drink the water of life
Reborn.

LETTER 16

Disappointment, imagined not seen

Beloved

This thorny clasp of the heart is here to stay until you see what you thought happened, didn't.
Who are you to say the world has to be your way.

When you look at him, do you see him, or do you see another? While putting this veil over their body, you stopped seeing clearly.

The night is in the midst, so hush now.

DISAPPOINTMENT

Bitter ripples circle my core
I avoid the encore
Yet it doesn't leave
Scratches at the door

Like a stray dog in the bare winter
Wincing a hushed hope
For warmer insides

What a blistering cold you left behind
Toes numb, glassy eyes
Afraid the glass will crack if I blink twice

I keep my eyes open and my door locked
I listen to that dog
Or is it now a wolf?
Howling with no moonlight in sight

Angry clouds gather above my house
Thunder rebukes my unforgiving heart
I dare to look outside and see
I left the gate open
To wildebeest and dragons alike

But there's no-one outside
Except my shadow
Against my window light
Imagined beings on a cold winter night.

LETTER 17

Beloved

I died in many ways.

I died in my mind, when I couldn't comprehend why I can't stop my thoughts. I died in my heart, when I couldn't stop the feelings invading my cells. I died in silence, when speaking was unnecessary. I died in love, when there were no more boundaries to keep. A good death?

I died in defeat, when greed beat common sense and we elected criminals to rule our world. I died in shame, when women shamed other women for being women. I died in my sleep, when reality was too heavy to bare. I died in my body a few times, when it was time for me to return.
A bad death?

There is nothing better than dying before dying, when there is no-thing left to take with me, except the love given and received.

Without the past, I am reborn in every moment. I could have been dead, and I am reborn now.

DEATH

Death is nothing but a gate to walk through
So you can be reborn once more

Everyday
Through every sound of your name on their lips
Through every memory touching their hearts
Through every picture held by longing hands
Through every time you visit them, they cry
But it's only love, so strong, we call it grief
We get confused, we humans, by love and death

Death is nothing but a gate you walk though
No one can ever leave us

Maybe just for a blink of an eye.

LETTER 18

Beloved

Wisdom is not a nicely drafted philosophy, words on a page that we hold on to at all costs. That's fundamentalism.

But an ever-changing insight that extends into our actions, embodied into the way we relate to ourselves and others.

WISDOM

Wisdom is a guest hosted by the mind overnight, travelling farther again each day.
It comes from a deeper place where words don't reach.
It travels light with no luggage of beliefs.
It knocks at the front door of the mind, but always enters through the back garden where there's space.

When the mind fears having an empty house, it tries to bribe the guest to stay longer.
If that doesn't work, it puts barriers at the exit.
It tries to shrink its revelations into conclusions, turning treasures from the deepest seas into a penny in the pocket.
Dresses the ego in spiritual clothing.
Binges on making ideas out of insights, gaining weight from the junk food of knowing and righteousness.
But wisdom whispers, that nothing can be held on to.
Nothing is final and absolute.
It always discovers itself over and over.

Being clever got you to the door, but not on the path.
All the books you read, the behaviours you predicted, results you earned, sins you got away with.
Still none the wiser.
Still gazing at the sky with a heart the size of a flea, crushed by the inability to live the truth you foretasted.

Wisdom is not a nicely drafted idea.

Not a sum of criteria of who you should be.
Who others should be to you.
Not a teaching of your understanding to others, but a mere walk to the limits of their own understanding.
Not grasping to conclusions in the name of morals, but diving into endless possibilities of life.
Not telling others to do that which you cannot do.

Wisdom is soft but enduring and alive.
It warms the wind in the sails of your forgiveness.

LETTER 19

Beloved

Kindness is the heart's song. If you ask your heart not to sing, and the bird not to fly, the wave not to wash the shore, then you wouldn't have lived at all.

What sorrow must be in the hearts that couldn't sing when it mattered. What heaviness to take to the other side.

And it only matters when there's no audience.

Sing when you're alone. Hurry.

KINDNESS

When you're kind to others in the daylight, but cruel to
yourself at night, you're not kind.

When you're kind only to some and not to others, your
kindness doesn't come from the heart.
You're making coins of the mind to buy you
righteousness.

If you're only kind to strangers, you're after redemption.
You're not kind.
If you're only kind to your family, you're after love.
You're not kind.
If you're only kind to your work, you're after glory.
You're not kind.
If you're only kind to lovers, you're after warranties.
You're not kind.

And the most unkind is when you couldn't be kind to
those who were kindest to you, even when they mustn't.

In the last night of your last day on earth, when there's
no one there to clap
The kindness you have withheld from yourself will rise
like a tidal wave
And not even the mountain of grief you've tenaciously
built will be able to retain it.

And then you will be at last washed in kindness.
But you would have run out of days.

LETTER 20

Beloved

Giving and Receiving is not a transaction, or a trade, but the dance of an inhale and exhale.

Don’t hold your breath in fear.

GIVING AND RECEIVING

When you give a little of something you have alot of,
and you do it for recognition, it's a tarnished gift.
When you give from obligation or duty,
you're not giving at all, but just trading.
When you give of your material possessions,
but not of yourself, you give nothing,
as tomorrow you may possess nothing.
But, when you have a little and give alot,
your riches never empty.

Some give looking for joy, and some give to erase pain,
or just give with an afterthought.
Yet giving when you have nothing to gain
is the biggest giving of all.
For when you give the way
the sun gives light to the horizon,
it's the giving that comes through you but not from you.

You don't labour the gift, you just pass it on.
And you never tire of this giving.

Only in giving of the mind from a drought of heart you tire.

And when a gift is offered with motive
but not received, then all loose.
When a gift is only half offered,
then it's not worthy of receiving.

And what is better than finding someone to receive
the gift you so much want to offer.
Because in giving,
the receiving itself is the gift of your fulfilment.
And so, in giving we receive and in receiving we give.

LETTER 21

Beloved

My word is my saviour and my executioner. My best friend and worst enemy. The bearer of light and shadow.

What a faithful servant to all there is.

Her mother, silence, cradles and nurtures the magic in her with a quiet devotion.

With word we go beyond word and without words we come back into this world.

THE WORD

There from the very beginning
Nothing made that was made without it

Yet never enough alone.
Just enough to spark dust into gold
Earth into fruit
To feed the man whose lips the word has spoken

Yes, darkness could not overcome it
Still, both in light and shadow it can move you

In joy or sadness,
In love or fear,
In hate or indifference

Or piety
Or reverence
Or gluttony
Spoken or unspoken
It carries the burden of our souls
With no complaints
But silence

And by its absence
It comforts your hearing
With the sound of the beginning
All the way through
to the end of your world.
The Word.

LETTER 22

Beloved

When I came here, I was pure and as soon as I opened my eyes I was scared.

I was born with no knowledge, then I was given knowledge. It kept adding up and piling up. So high it cast a shadow on all else that wasn't knowledge.

I had to forget so I can remember.

I remembered and it was so long ago like it was yesterday.

It seemed smaller than knowledge but when I looked from beyond, it kept all the knowledge inside it, like a hand.

My joy, I was in it and I touched its fingers.

JOY

Original state, yet forever fleeting
Slipping through wrinkled fingers
Of yesterdays's tomorrow.
Hiding in crevices of memories:

Bird songs, sun light
Breeze on skin, salty hair
Toes in warm sand

Hot drink in the cold
Extra blanket at night
Raindrops on the window

Smell of fresh bread in the morning
Laughter of someone you love
A hug, a hold.
Holding on.
And when these are gone
Your joy is gone.
But look inside, look again
Look deeper to find
That Joy was at home already
The hostess of all guests,
Holding your soul's mirror
Pointing it at the sun
Reflecting you into the world.

LETTER 23

Love, not all you need, but all you are.

Beloved

A tiny ray of light started to flicker in your chest. It's thin as a hair but still you feel it.
It reaches farther than light and asks for nothing.
If you let it, it will grow bigger.
If you don't let it, it will still grow bigger.
But if you oppose, it will hurt until you allow it.
Because no matter where you're heading, there is just one destination and one origin.

Who will get there first?

LOVE

Love is not all you need.
Not a feeling you latch on.
Not a passing cloud on the sky of your emotions.
Not a prize to get that makes everything worthwhile.
If I get love, then I will be whole.
If I feel love, then I will have lived.
But where are You?
Show love where to find you.
Forge the tools of truth from the fire in your belly
Cool it in the thirst of your heart
Sharpen it in the corners of your mind
Then when love comes knocking
Your hands may unlock the door.
And if you're going to Love
Love how
The Dark loves the Light
The Sky loves the Sea
The Sun loves the Moon
Apart yet always together
The Sun lights up the Moon
And the Moon makes the Sun the centre of the world.
Maybe when we sleep, they lay-down, side by side
In the field beyond knowing
Past the valley of understanding
Where only the word reaches.
That's where Love may find you too
And then its truth will knock down
the chains of all your fears
And you will see who loved
You first.

LETTER 24

Beloved

I was looking for peace everywhere else. Not where it was. I strived and tried and it was nowhere to be found. As soon as I thought I grabbed it by one foot, it would escape.
I finally gave up, gave in.

I woke up one average morning and when my feet touched the ground I felt it. The joy. And with it came my long-lost friend.

It was everywhere.

PEACE

Glimmering sand caressing your fingers
Cool sea water quivering your chest
Warmth of sun stroking your shoulders
And the heart swimming in peace.

Crisp winter air carrying youth to your face
Crystal snowflakes molten your skin
Warm scarf embracing your neck
And the mind breathing in peace.

Old wounds of past now precious gems
Adorning a life that raised you
To be the treasure you are today
And your soul dancing with peace.

LETTER 25

Truth, not a definition, but a cosmos

Beloved

When you had enough of the world and wanted your truth told, where did you go?
Who wants to hear your truth with no judgment?
What is the mind for, if not for judging.
And when you said it, spoke it, lived it - the truth - what was your reward? None. You got punished, so you forced your truth on others instead, and got hit by the might of your arrogance.
Truth has no material reward, but life itself.

Rest now.

TRUTH

My truth and yours
Like night and day
Both real in their way

Try to make mine yours?
Twilight cannot pause
Stirs the light away

To a place beyond time
Where your truth and mine
Like stardust entwine

Into one single speck
Unsaid, unseen, unfound
Dark matter of fact

Eternally magnetised
Into Now.

LETTER 26

Beloved

The madness is deep. I have a thought, I churn it, if I don't like the outcome, I replace it with another. Some thoughts are older, I've grown them into ideas. I latch onto them and you and I, we run the world by way of thought extremism.

But no thought is ever the truth. And when a thought arises, it doesn't need to occupy all my insides. I can choose to go deeper. When I travel inwards deep enough, the thoughts may or may not disappear, but they will begin to reflect my depth, more often than they reflect my surface.

By pure means of gravity, my inner depth will start pulling my thoughts inwards. Not to make them vanish or destroy them, but hold them into a loving embrace.

My thoughts are no longer my enemy. I didn't start them, so I can't stop them. I don't need to.

The mind becomes a trusted friend, always pointing to where my centre of gravity is. Whispering to look deeper into soul.

The soul is the thought's longing. Mind can only think it, but I must search to find it.

THINKING

Thoughts long for the soul
Devoted to showing the way
Like moss on trees pointing north

But the traveller decides which direction to take
Sometimes south seems the best bet
The long way around the back of your head

It has to be that way
Wake up from thinking into being
Where thoughts plug into your centre,
Not your perception

There is no new thought in the world
We all recycle each other's nightmares
But there is a new life in each of us

That feeds everything, holds everything
Beyond thought form
Beyond senses

It's always there so we tend to forget it.
Like we forget we're being breathed
Blink and you will miss it

LETTER 27

Beloved

I was told not to hear the sound of the heart against my ribcage. I was told to only listen to reason and cut off the thread between them.

Thread so fine like a ray of light interrupted by speckles of dust that rise out of nowhere, creating little shapes of undetermined naming or convention. Surrounded by miniature rainbows that make no sense. Why is there a rainbow around a dust speck?

I don't know what the mind is supposed to do with all this, so I just stop seeing rainbows, of all sorts and shapes.
I just think about water being broken in various angles of future possibilities. I calculate the area of the triangle.

And I am left feeling empty.

FEELING

My body has a language
Of undetermined convention
No names can be found
In dictionaries of sharp minds
Ruling the world of words
And concepts and philosophies

Unfounded in nothing but the past
A bank of images
That left traces on your retina
And got catalogued as
'Return to sender'
Recipient is no longer at home.

Yet this body keeps talking
In languages of other worlds
Uncatalogued
So therefore left unattended
On the desk of
A really busy person
Busy arriving to the end of the line
Whatever that line is
Once crossed,
I can't go back
For another chance
To open letters
In invisible envelopes
By unnamed senders

LETTER 28

Beloved

If a thought comes to me and I take it as the truth, I become a believer. When I become a believer, the world may see me as determined, driven, set for accomplishments.

But what if when I become a believer, I also become a slave? Slave to my own thoughts, which I arrogantly take as being True. Ideologies kill.

What if when I don't know anything for sure, I regain the innocence and curiosity of a child?

What if that is the only way to end division? Looking at truth from outside my personal beliefs.

Would I rather be a believer or a not knower?

BELIEVING

I believe in right and wrong
And endings and beginnings
Sun rising and setting on my mind
Still churning my origins

I believe in love and hate
One is better than the other
Both absolve you of crimes
In sight of judges with no eyes

I believe in me, whoever I may be
A stranger or a friend, the same
I know I can only be
That which you can see

I believe it's all imagined
Says another fainted voice
And I don't want to challenge
Because it doesn't hurt

The only truth I know
Is clear
Of pain and suffering my dear

LETTER 29

Beloved

What is that knowing, no book has it, no wise one can speak it.
It only speaks to you, in tongues only you understand.
If you trust it, it saves lives.
And sometimes it seems to be a little bit crazy, but have faith in your body as it holds keys to doors you didn't even know existed.

Trust the moon light. Even when it's cloudy, it shines.

INSIGHT

Delight
Of night
No sight
Or freight
Just right.
No fight
Or flight
Just light.
It might
Be slight
No spotlight
No daylight
But alright,
Like torchlight
Gives sight.
You alight
In fire-flight
With insight,
Your birthright.

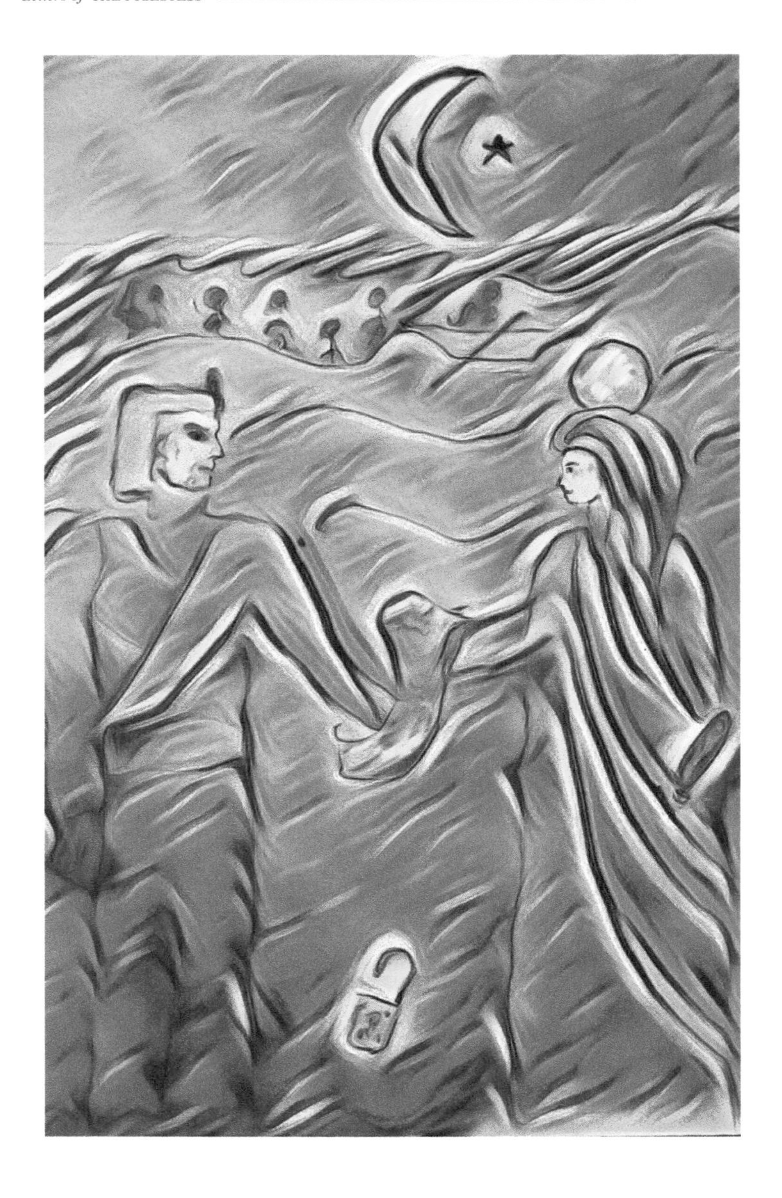

The Tide Rises Once More

The sea around the prison tower is far from calm. The moon spins her face and pulls a large wave hitting the guard's chambers. Although he is still frightened, he now understands the way of the moon as he has seen it with his own eyes. He is prepared and takes the Priestess through the fifth gate. The locks don't work here, so he will have to watch her awake.
To stay awake, he will be reading her letters. And some, he will take to the people on the shore during his daily trip. He has grown fond of reading, as the High Priest never let him read.

The Priestess hands him letters.

He takes her words into his world.

LETTER 30

Beloved

Some values come to me from the mind. They fleet and melt like snow on the tip of my tongue. And other values come from the soul. And those I can't even name.

I can make up goals and achieve them and get recognition. But if my soul doesn't agree with who I must become in the name of achievement, then my life will be as dry as the desert and no oasis will quench my thirst.

I may die rich with eulogies carved in gold, yet my resting place will be lonelier than a rose in the Sahara.

Being who I am is the only way to be with the One I am with.

VALUES

My deepest values, I can't name
They hover over the tip of my tongue
Anchored somewhere I can't see,
Not even ancestry can root in there

I say I value truth and I stay hidden
What do I value?
I claim I value love and act in guilt
What do I value?
I swear I value freedom and chain myself
What do I really value?

My deepest values, I can't name
They move me silently into becoming
Spinning invisible life threads
Into the cloth of my making

LETTER 31

Beloved

If there is ever a challenge, the biggest one is to remain that which I am at my deepest. No matter what I have to lose or gain. Especially when I have everything to lose, integrity is the spine of who I am.

The reward is unmeasurable. I know I can't be broken because what I am is unbreakable.

So then, I am not afraid to bend with the wind.

Integrity is not rigid, it's fluid like water. It goes from vapour to liquid to ice, but it doesn't disappear. It just transforms, remaining fundamentally the source of life.

INTEGRITY

You feed the soul like rain feeds earth
Making green leaf grow through stone
In any shape, you don't mind the form
You remain what you are, break the norm:

Clouds, carriers of life above
Vapours, endless exhales of trees
Fog, feeding leaves in open cold
Rainy mist for thirsty roots
Ice, keeper of life beyond time
Snow, blanket of white for sleeps to come
River flood, breaking barriers too high
Making its way to Waves,
In Seas and Oceans where everything is born again
New and ancient
All the same,
It remains
Itself

Be like water

LETTER 32

Masculine, the muscle of the heart
Feminine, the blood that pumps through

Beloved

I have in me, as with the world, a divine part of structure holding the architecture of life together. The masculine. And this structure exists so there is a grounding to anything that may wish to come into this world, through me. That is the feminine.

A book without the words filling it, is not a book. Water with no vessel, inundates and spills. The masculine and feminine are sacred in their own way but indestructible as One.

No good has come from separating them and giving them ranks. During dark nights of Ego, both have taken turns to try and run my world, and each time a new plague has arisen, from this distortion.

Could my body be the house where they become One?

MASCULINE AND FEMININE

Books without pages
Empty vessels
For thirsty mouths
Lives built on sand of promises
Of that which we are not
Lost meanings of sacred
Confused by the inertia
Of order and control
Criminals in charge of justice
Thieves in charge of our home
Mothers selling their breast
To feed sons that grow to learn
That selling yourself is a way to earn
We strive hungry and thirsty
Threading waters in the dark
And we don't know how to swim
We were never taught
Somehow we learn to float
We sense the truth holding the
Molecules of water
That holds us,
That washes us
And we don't even need to struggle
We can just let the breath
Enter our lungs.
Knowing we will be reunited
Once more

LETTER 33

Beloved

What would it be like if we would practise devotion towards each other, instead of negotiating our shortcomings? What if instead of keeping scores, we would keep each other in highest regard? Not as compensation, but as a way of being.

And instead of wanting to be understood, we would first wish to understand.

Unguarded, undivided, devoted to being.

DEVOTION

For lifetimes I could:

Make you soup
To feed your soul
Cover you with blankets of love
To thaw your heart

Hold your head on my bosom at night
While you're dreaming our tomorrow

Rapture in your ravishing
Enfold you in soft insides
Let my rivers flow to your ocean
My day kiss the forehead of your night

For your fire lights me up like a thousand suns
And threshes me into stardust
Then melts me into gold
Forges me into the sacred cup
You hold with your hands
Touch with your lips
Fill up with each sip
Each breath
Everyday
For lifetimes

LETTER 34

Beloved

I know there's a place where we can meet as we are. Where neither need nor want are present.
I can't wait for you to stop needing me so we can finally love each other.

RULES

There's this place
Not so far
Between my nevers and your shoulds
Where the grass doesn't need rain to grow
The sky doesn't need blue to amaze
Your mind doesn't need me to feel worthy
And my heart doesn't need you
To feel loved
There's this place
It's not far

LETTER 35

Beloved

I have separated the sacred and the flesh, as if sacred chooses by judgement that which it will live in.
Yet it is the desire in the flesh that created life and isn't life sacred?
There is a sacred fire lit inside our wombs and groins, yet we tarnish it with religion and we turn it to crime with scruples and taboos.
What of the sacred touch of life that only two lovers can ignite?
What of the mountains and fields that will yield to your love making?
Next to love, sexual energy is the most powerful there is, that is Creation through Union, with or without the flesh.

EROTIC

You don't need a school of Tantra
To touch me into bliss
Nor do you need to search the books
For angles and techniques
You only need to read between the lines of my
Valleys and my hills
Get high on the scent of my skin
Pause for a sip
You lost your breath
Don't worry I found it
It is resting on my breast
This is not a test, time has stopped
Hearts beating an encore
Just slow it down some more
Don't worry about a thing
There is more time than you think
If it looks like it's gone when I leave
Feel twice when you close your eyes
My touch will still light up your sky
And I don't even try,
I might die
And if I do,
it's only for touching
you

LETTER 36

Beloved

I have a shadow or two. One is dark and it likes to hide from the world, the other is too bright for the world. Either way I hide my shadows.

I try to wash them down with holy water, burn them in incandescent letters, chase them out with burning myrrh smoke.

But it doesn't work. I can't get myself out of myself. One night in my dream my shadow found me. I held it in an embrace. It was all it ever wanted, to be held.

Receive your shadow and watch it illuminate you brighter than you can ever imagine.

SHADOW

Shadow is a form of light
Or is light a form of darkness?
Darkness condensed to matter
Weighty combustion of beliefs

Particles so close together
Edges blur into forgotten scenes
Black and Gold dancing in your sleep
What is there not to keep?

Shame rises in my dreams
As innocent creatures
I hold closer, I nurture
Until they say no to self-torture

Shadows fill my light
Breathing air on the embers of my fire
Burning longer deeper stronger
My body now an incandescent amplifier

LETTER 37

Beloved

I was so stuck in my idea, even life itself came out of the barricades to show me my delusions. Still, I didn't want to change my mind. Even Reality best die before my Ego. I am what I think I am, so how can I cause my own death? I am too scared, so I will hold on to my beliefs. That will keep me safe, keep me alive…Or will it?

I have lived by others and done all that I was asked to do.

So who am I Really? If I am what I Do and Do what others want me to, am I Them? In a way we all are each other, but in this other way, the very loud internal way - I can only be me, a part only I can exist in. And if I drown this part or make it a secret, I can never fully live. I will disconnect from the source of life itself, just to look alive but be dead. What a delusion of all delusions.

I can't unplug myself from Me and still exist inside. I can certainly look the part. I can fool everyone, but I can't fool myself.

How endearingly 'cruel to be kind' from life to offer Reality, over and over again.

DELUSION

It's so cold in the desert tonight
Embers drawing final breaths
I hear sounds of distant creatures
Their names I've never met

If I sleep I hope to dream
Of lush oases full of green
And clear water and dancers
Wearing colourful dresses
Feeding me answers

It's dark now too, the fire is stone
Stars seem closer than home
I've been away for so long
I can't remember who was wrong

I keep travelling places
Building tents into spaces
With no gates or roofs
Moving my home into others

Who cares if it's not real
I'll keep dreaming it until dawn

LETTER 38

Beloved

Of all the human fears, I dread regret the most.

This silent enemy with no weapons, hides in all corners, thrives on drought but doesn't need the sun to grow. It grows in the dark alone, expands with time.

You can't fight what you can't see and sometimes it will stay with you and fight. But you won't see it clearly. You may be smiling on the outside but how harsh you may look on the inside.

Sometimes you won't know why and other times you will be certain, yet there is no going back.

The darkest teacher, regret.

Regret

You're like a thistle
Sticking to woollen clothes
Not even water washes you out
Sacrifice my garment, it's the only way out

You're so bitter
My mind makes my tongue believe you're sweet
Otherwise my heart would forget to beat
You follow me everywhere even in my dreams
I wake up cold, bursting at the seams

Regret, my worst enemy

Be gone
"No, I am here to wake you up"
Leave
"No, I am here to remind you of your choices"
Go away
"No, I am here because you cannot go against your heart
And not meet me"

I only stick to rough surfaces
Best polish all you have
Or stick with me until the end

LETTER 39

"Anything or anyone that leaves me, it's for a better life"
Byron Katie

Beloved

No one can ever abandon me, but myself.

Even if I was a small child in a basket, left at someone's doorstep, I would still encourage my eyes to see my parent was honest. They knew they couldn't do me justice. No matter how asleep they seemed, they knew.

And who can leave the one inside me, other than the infinite occupier and sole inhabitant of my body? Me.

I beg, don't give so much ownership of your life to others. Don't be so arrogant to believe other people's lives only revolve around you.

None of us could live in someone else's shoes, for 5 minutes. And if we tried, it's only because of righteousness, not because of compassion.

When I abandon myself, the whole world cries with me.

ABANDON

The apple tree doesn't stop flowering
Because there was ice last winter
It doesn't keep a grudge on snow
Nor does it cry for being frozen
Or wind blowing its leaves

It reaches deeper with its roots
Turns sap into sprouts
Looks towards the sun
Makes light into green
Heat into fruit
Drinks rain and dances rhythms of breeze
With its best friend summer

When Autumn comes
you take the sweetest bite
It doesn't ask you to pay
For picking its long cared for fruit
And then enjoying it all winter

It goes and repeats it again every year
Frozen, blown by wind and burnt by sun
For that's how the fruit is made
The apple tree makes apples
no matter what you think.

LETTER 40

Beloved

I doubted myself. Every moment, even when I knew that was my best self. I doubted. I looked at others and saw my fears. What would they think about my best?
Oh, how I hurt myself believing: I am wrong and I need to un-wrong myself.
I so believed in it, I was willing to hurt others for my redemption. I was willing to hurt myself for my redemption. I was willing to let everything die except my ego, my 'I'.

But most painful, I was willing to let my own truth die for my value in the eyes of others. If sin is being off the mark, I missed it. I missed my mark.

Heartbreak lets the light in.

REDEMPTION

When the faith's clock strikes twelve
Your eardrum bleeds oppression
From the sound of the question:
What can save me from sin?

And what is sin?
But a moment of doubt
When you saw yourself checkout
Less than worthy, a sell out

When you believed a story, over Life
You reduced your soul to strife
And sold your life for one single action
And now you want to buy back a fraction
But it's all sold out

Who would you be without the story of sin?

And if you decide to believe in sin
And trade life to buy redemption
Why doesn't it even begin
To wash away
The pain
The despair you gave yourself everyday

Maybe it's because
You're yet to see

That life can never be a trade
But every day a chance anew
To see yourself
Beyond what you do
Something brighter than your eyes can take
You're guilty only of heartbreak
For believing in sin

LETTER 41

Beloved

I was overtaken by holy anger. The one that drives everything to change. The world has become blatantly distorted by gaining riches and control over other human beings. Over how they move and even how they feel. Over who is seen as powerful, yet they have no idea what power is. Frightened they use force instead. To create hierarchies to sustain greed. None of this will be taken on the other side so what's the rush to looking so accomplished. What even is accomplishment, what is achievement? On whose scale do you base your life upon? Whose beliefs are you dragging along?

We put a price on everything even the unmeasurable and sacred.

Your selflessness is the sheep's clothing onto the wolf of your lost worthiness.

Rest. You are enough. There is enough in the world for everyone.

Be safe in your nakedness.

Ego in God's Clothing

Oh you, so righteous, you have gone adrift!

Took the word, turned into judgements
The holy made it the juror
The divine the executioner
You imprisoned your soul
Inside the highest church
Guarded by Saints and Martyrs
Two-faced angels from hell

You went blind praising a God
Through other's eyes
How futile when you have your own eyes
You even labelled love itself:
Too young, too old
Too gay, too lesbian
Too interracial
Keep the married married
And the unmarried unmarried
Because nothing matters more
Than your fabricated justice

But the sin of your ignorance
Your children will pay for
Until the end of time.

When you go out
Into the final night
The truths revealed
Will be too late to comfort.
Alone, they will take on
The ragged outfit
To pass it to their own

You know God?
You read the holy books
And pray beads?
And when you're done
You violate your soul with ethics
And tell yourself
You know right from wrong

Impostor

You live to drag the past into the future
Loyal to long gone you
Neither dead, nor alive anymore
Flogging other dead along the way
For tradition!

Coward

I feel the mighty anger rising,
The clearing fire of all delusions
I want to grasp the sword of truth
And strike

But then God whispers as your breath
Holds your heart in sacred rhythm
So you can rise again
For another chance to become naked
Start again
You wake up and spit God in the eyes
One more time
And that's when I have to love you, She said

LETTER 42

Beloved

I was innocent because I believed my thoughts. If we believe, we are like children dreaming. I do not know anything else about reality, other than what I hold in my beliefs.
And if I see a dreamer, I mustn't wake him.
I only need to look at my own illusions.
Until there is nothing left to forgive.

FORGIVENESS

The boulder chained at the back of your middle
Is tied by the thoughts you weaved around it
Millions of threads
knotted in beliefs
tangled in memories
secured in expectations
shoved under the ribs to your left.
Breathe.
And then question.
Are you a believer?
And when you blindly believe, you're unconscious
And when you're unconscious, you do not know
And when you do not know, you're Innocent.
Even at the darkest hour when they meant it
They did not really know.
For no one knows all the corners and cracks of your soul,
Even you.
They are innocent, as are you.
Cut the soft chains of your load
With the sword of truth.
And if you still can't forgive
Pray you are forgiven for your convictions
Then receive the jewels your offender has left you
And become the richest on Earth, and in Heaven.

PART III
OF THE OTHER WORLD

LETTER 43

Beloved

Don't be afraid of silence. It's where everything comes from. Even when everything is loud, silence is still there, patient. In everything told and untold. Even if you don't want silence, silence wants you.

Silence isn't empty, or full, but rich.
Rich of everything.

SILENCE

What's asking to rise on your lips
What's stirring in your waking

Waves of the untold
drowning on the shore

Treacle steps through burning sand
Thirsting for the ocean

Questions dare not ask
Peaking out like rocks
You want to dive from

Deeper
Darker
Closer to the end of the world

What's that sound?

Is it being born?
Drumming at your ribcage
Is it dying?
Pulsating your heart in its hand
Wait.
Is that you?
You sound like silence

LETTER 44

The Unspoken, silent but loudly alive.

Beloved

I was startled from a deep sleep. I fell and fell into a darkness that engulfed me. But I wasn't cold. It was warm and embracing. I didn't know what to do other than let it have me. I was numb yet alive, like never before. My skin caught fire then went cold and my edges blurred.

What if I'm not afraid anymore?

THE UNSPOKEN

The sound of words unborn
Lives in the place
Where the dark light shines
Behind the mountains underneath the sun
Where dreams untold
And hopes forgotten are cast away.

Outside fire, inside ice
Search for holy ground
Fall in the abyss of unknown
Be startled and woken
Finally dive I say
And in this dry, black sea
The echo of the first sigh of the world
Reverberates on your skin.

Hush loudly at the edge of emptiness
Shhhhh
and abiding in your deafness
feel the unspoken
come alive

LETTER 45

"When I look inside and see that I am Nothing, that's Wisdom. When I look outside and see that I am Everything, that's Love. And between these two my life turns"
Nisargadatta Maharaj

Beloved

What is this imperceivable movement, like invisible pendulums oscillating inside my ribcage?

I turn my face to the left and right and all I see is dark and light flashing to the core of my soul, making my eyes close tighter than the gates of fear.

I am afraid I will get lost if I open my eyes.

It's so bright in here. I am afraid to shine.

INWARD AND OUTWARD

Inward, a moist moving night
No fingers on hands, no grasp
You swim-fly in this ocean-space
Dissolving
with no choice of opposing
Vanishing

Outward, scorching idle day
Buzzing sounds of life
You hold on to, hold, hug
Nothing escapes you
All begets you
Merging

Turn in-between like a pendulum
With rhythm of breath
Don't hang too long
In your day or night
Or you'll get lost
And miss
Life

LETTER 46

Beloved

What is being to you? I know what it isn't. When you abdicated ownership of your actions. You were just being yourself when you hurt someone, but there is still a need to make amends. Not for who you are, but for your ignorance of who they are. What did you miss of them, when you were too busy looking at yourself?

Stay the same and look at your part.

Just being, isn't ignoring the elephant in the room, waiting for it to pass by. Just being could mean no outside action at first, but on the inside everything moves so fast, it looks still.

All being leads to becoming.

Being

The image you present to others
Is rotted around the edges
From lingering into stale waters
Of meaningless self-reference

You're afraid of being empty of illusions
Because the emptiness seems dark
And the void seems cold
So at least you can hold on to your false self
But it doesn't make you warm

And there is nothing darker than
A deep soul choosing to live in the shallow
Appreciation of public achievements and
Moral righteousness, the ego's trap
For in one single moment
The deepest whisper in you
May reach your ears
And then you may allow yourself to feel
Empty
Dark
Empty of lies
Dark of illusion
Full of an invisible colourless nameless
otherworldly
Being

Live from there if you dare

LETTER 47

Beloved

I tried and tried and failed so many times.
Achieving goals doesn't work in matters of the spirit. How can you find something you have never seen before, something beyond experience. It doesn't make sense because it is beyond senses.

There is another sense, with no external device. Something that knows it knows and it knows it doesn't know, something that can hold everything as it is, without changing itself like emotions or like thoughts change, like beliefs change, like season change. It doesn't move, yet it's everywhere.

This is what I seek and the seeking is maybe futile, but it takes me to the edge of my mind.

I want to see if I can dive from it, in it.

SEEKING

I will not go there with you
The seeker told me, one early morning
Hours, days spent together, planning
Our journey of fire and ice

I don't have supplies or compass
I will die at sea in the storm, I can't swim
I will look at the stars trying to find North
And I will miss all the other stars

I will not go there with you
The seeker says, repeating the mantras
Sat on the mat praying, with mudras
And chants and crystal bowls

I will stay here inside, safe from harm
Trying to find the centre of life
From outside of it, or around it
Yes, I will go around it to find it.

Ok you fool, I said, stay here inside
I am going out in the storm
I'd rather die and be reborn
Shattered in stardust again
I will be out in the cold
Until it finds me or strikes me
Either way, I'd rather live
Than seeking that you cannot seek

LETTER 48

Beloved

If I ever do something, although nothing can be done unto oneself, it would be to unsee everything I have been shown.

All ideas of right and wrong, of what love is and isn't, of how I should wear my garment in front of others.

Of what I am or my soul is, the definitions given to things that cannot be defined. Boundaries set on unbounded hearts.

That is what I wish to unsee.
As my mind in its beauty can find everything that it has ever seen.

UNSEEING

Close your eyes
Let yourself be blind
See nothing except nothingness

Don't be afraid of darkness
Let your sight turn sideways
And see from one single eye
In your chest or everywhere

Except in your mind
You can't unsee by way of thoughts
They keep you trapped in places
Where memories save faces
Of things to be unseen

Don't be afraid to die before your death
You're more than memories imprinted in cells.
You're more than a body with eyes
You're that which you are not
And that which you are Now,
Let go of your Before.

LETTER 49

Beloved

This part was treacherous. A rocky mountain, muddy paths, slanted narrow crossings with no vantage point.
Sleet and ice then scorching sun burning flesh and ground alike. All my senses left me.

Until I reached a stream, the water so clear and I followed it. It grew larger into a river that took me to its bank full of lush green grass and a breeze that dried all my wounds and my cuts turned into scabs and they fell.

I had no more clothes so I just jumped into the river and washed my new found body. The mountain looked peaceful in the distance.

PURGE

My body is like a mountain
The crest is scalded by the sun
Yet covered in snow and ice
Not many get to meet this place
And those who do
Will not dwell here
As this place is only mine

The middle is sometimes barren
Other times has a bit of green
But all the time it has caves
With riches or nothingness alike
Coals to burn fires of hearts
Precious gems to ornate arms
If you can dig that far down that is

When you reach the valleys
You get to drink the purest water
It cleanses your soul
Of all you thought was wrong in you
But there was nothing wrong
Just seasons of life embracing
A mountain that stands tall
Descending bodies growing naked
Into a winter's snow

LETTER 50

Beloved

Go up and see what holds everything together.
But don't abide there, come back down.

Transcending alone is not changing the world. Bring back down what you found there.

Allow it to move the world through its descent.

TRANSCEND

So much of the world in one go
Makes you want to pack your bags, I know
Travel to a place, not traced on any maps
Except that time you marked the spot with an X
Where your mind, heart and body briefly met

And it was so beautiful, you wanted to stay
You keep looking for it since, everyday
It had something that held you, weightlessly
Beauty of rainbows made effortlessly
No rain required
Just the light of so many suns dancing
On floors of infinite seas of colours unseen
And you join in, without arms or legs you move
Your chest radiates from light pulsating
On beats unheard before, composed by you
And you can't remember, was it September
Memories don't work here
There is nothing to prove, you just move

As soon as you don't want it to end, it ends
Prepare for your descent
Let your flesh make it real
Bring that beat to the ground
To grow new sounds
For old ears
And eyes full of tears
Of joy and hope

LETTER 51

Beloved

This body is not my only form. I live through it, but there is something else surrounding it. There is something in it that I cannot see or touch or fit through the gates of my senses. Something that no wise person can capture, no matter what technology they use.

There is something bigger that doesn't fit in the confinement of my organs so it expands and gets bigger, like a house, housing this body. And there is a bigger house housing all our bodies, from this world and all the worlds.

I don't know what colour it is, but it is of a bright glow.

Like the full moon on a clear sky.

SOUL

You travelled down the ladder of life
Into a small right ventricle
Pulsating a beat like a near rhyme
With no ideas of ethical
Just a thirst and hunger
Of joy
Of life
Of breath

You grow bigger each day, each inhale
Make room for whatever was to come
Like a gentle host of everyone
With platters of smiles and embraces
No judgements
Just caresses
Of love
Of acceptance

You kept growing like daylight onto night
There is no doubt you've been here before
Through other hearts and eyes, an encore
No need to worry
About endings
It's an open ended story
Your soul

LETTER 52

Beloved

What does it look like? You showed me once long ago but I can't remember.
I forgot.
Lost amongst pictures of how not to be.

What would it be like to see each other as equals, as souls breathing the same air, made from the same dust, in the same universe?

Whether a man or woman or a gender unspecified being, because they can specifically hold both equally, having their heart bigger than most conventional imaginations.

What is it like to be simply divine?

DIVINE

Protector of life
Gatekeeper of love
Provider of freedom
Bringing riches unmeasured by coins

To be as you are fully
You live in all there is

You hold us in warmest embrace
Wise beyond books
Sage beyond any age
Warrior against fear
Hunter of shadows

Healer of all wounds
Bridge of underworlds
Nurturer of souls
Creating worlds unbounded by borders

To be as you are fully
You live in all there is

You soothe the deepest wounds
Spark life into stone
Your touch turns anything to gold
Earth reborn when you breath
Heaven opens when you call

We are in all there is

LETTER 53

Beloved

I lived in a dream before. The worst dreams are not nightmares. With nightmares, you know you want to wake up.

But dreams where reality is hidden behind mundane averages and safe compromises. Those are the dangerous ones. Because they make us forget, they dull us down into a long sleep. One that no one can wake us up from.

When a baby's asleep, you don't want to wake them.
Only look at your own dreams and if you gonna dream, make it lucid dreaming.

I dream of lucid living.

DREAM

Dream, dream away child
Your pillow so light
Your heart's delight
Mind's eye in sight
Of treasures hunting grounds
Fear not waking up
If you fall deeper
You'll wake down
And fly high where bird song quivers
Swim with fins of gold in topaz rivers
Wings of light and legs of dragon
Will take you on seventh heaven's mountain
To turn stones into gems
And nightmares into fairy tales
You'll speak in tongues you won't remember
By December
But the world will catch you
If you dare to dream
Dream away
Gently I say
Don't wake the baby

LETTER 54

Beloved

I was looking for something outside of me, something to make contact and explain all the troubles of the world.
If this was a Father, I was angry at him, and if this was a Mother I would look down upon her. How is this all allowed?

Until I realised the world is I, and you. This playground has been given to us like a toy to a child from love of play and discovery. And sometimes the child loves a toy and other times they break it, even when they love it, they break it.

And their parents still offer them another, and another, and another chance.

Out of love.

GOD'A

Guilty for world's shortcomings,
For storms and sunshine alike
For time not stopping or too soon stopping.
Rests their feet on your hope and comfort

Hush a bit now and rest your mind
Touch the place where nothing moves
And sounds don't reach
Can you see God through the same eye
That God sees you

For they so loved you
They gave the world to you
A home to welcome yourself in

A perfect embrace of the first spark with its cradle
The sky to make a fire
To bring you life
To be joy
To be you
To be

LETTER 55

Beloved

I got this far and didn't write to you about Fear.

How funny. I always said we don't Do fear in this house. Fear doesn't live here. I rather be anything but a coward.

Look back only after she has passed.

FEAR

I will embrace my fear
Let it drain through my veins
Make my body tremble
Dry my mouth
Skip a beat of my heart
Make my hair rise
My voice shake
Take me to paths unknown
On a poorly lit night
Meet me face to face
On dark alleys
With dead ends

But I will not give fear
Authors rights to my life
Last say in a fight
Navigate my boat through storms
Or sleep on my bedroom floors
I will not look back
Until I have reached
My unseen shore
Where I drop my anchor
I've lost all the anger
Let my soul linger
In the sweet scent
Of freedom
From sailing through fear

LETTER 56

Beloved

All these times you tried and failed to let go. Can you now see that you cannot let go of it, but it lets go of you, once you receive it with all your heart and being?

I sat down on the stone path, did nothing. I just sat there being held by the ground. And it felt so safe. So peaceful.

When I got up, I was another.

SURRENDER

A silent thief on a moist night
Breaking and entering my home

It's not until the morning dawns
That I know:
All my belongings are gone

I didn't lose them.
I was robbed instead
Quietly, taken in the night

And just as I am about to start grieving
Over what I thought I needed
The corner of my left eye sees my home bigger and brighter than ever before

The stillness of my empty house
Dancing with all the things I hadn't touched in so long - gone

Dancing with the things I had been touching - gone

Whispering life onto new things I wanted to bring home
But there was no room.
Before I opened my other eye, it all let go of me.

Gone.

Then I woke up
And all things
Past, present and future
Right where they belong

LETTER 57

Beloved

I tried to fit in. They said if I do, my life will be easier and I wanted easy. The illusion of easy seemed to be the one to hold on to. Yet why was it so hard to be someone else? Why did it feel like void? Not the holy void, the other one. There are two voids. One that's full of life spark and one that sucks the life out of me.

Pain told me to try something else. And when I did, when I stepped off the long traded path by others, I carved my own.

And when I did, I saw others doing the same. And I was alone but I wasn't.

No one ever is.

ALONE

Stand as you are
Eyes bright
Heart light
No one to despair or delight

Root down alone
Like the tree in the Savannah
Offering shade like Nirvana
In infinite seeker heat
Too many lie to belong,
Disconnected
Hide to be accepted
Slouch under expectations invested
Offer compassion
But don't join them
Stand alone
Like the tree
Rooted down
With its crown high
Taking the sun
That others can't bear
Their skin too thin

I stand alone
Watching you
Standing
And alone we stand together

LETTER 58

Beloved

If you only ever choose the easiest way, the quick way out, you only increase your suffering. It's a shortcut to losing yourself.

All the teachings you've heard are worth nothing at all until lived. The idea of love is nothing compared to the act of love. And that's in the body.

EMBODY

Speak up, when it's easier to hush
Show up, when it's easier to hide
Listen, when it's easier to shout

Knock down the walls
Bricks of lies glued with fear
Hammer it down with your sight

Replace the books with actions
The teaching with wisdom
The idea of love with acts of love

Return to yourself
To the home long forgotten
Guarded by tall cedars
The trees of God
In the garden of your soul
Watered with love
That doesn't end
Warmed by the sun
That always rises
Relentless
In its shining.

LETTER 59

Beloved

I have seen the water rising higher and higher.
I have sensed my skin turn into scales. I held my breath.
I didn't swim, just floated and when I finally arrived and I met myself outside of myself, I recognised myself within.
With great thunder I receive my power, united with all that there is.
My words are my army, my pen is my protection, I offer you the same, to have and own.
Without force, only silence, the mother of all words.
In stillness it lives.

The moon has turned all tides to the top of the mountains.

Power

*P*owerful thunder before the storm alights
*O*pens the sky to everything, incites
*W*idens the horizon ready to bathe in fire
*E*ndures the hail storm of your words desire
*R*eborn from ashes, ember fins
*I*gnites the fire within
*S*alutes the goddess and her king
*I*ncandescent communion
*N*imbus holds your reunion
*Y*our seat in your kingdom awaits
*O*pen arms in longing embrace
*U*nited at long last

The Night At The Top Of The Tower

The stormy tides have passed and the water is clear as a mirror.

The world has heard the Priestess's voice through the faithful journey of the Guard. Word reached the High Priest that believers stopped believing. He dropped his robes into the sea and went free into the sunset.

The Priestess stands at the top of the tower. She can look down and sees the shore through shallow water. She could swim there if she wanted to. But she needn't do that yet. The Guard arrives at sunrise and he will take her on his boat.

One last night to bathe in moonlight.

THE END

EPILOGUE

WHEN PEOPLE SAW THE MOON'S FACE

When people saw the moon's face, they lit up like stars.
They remembered they had been stars themselves
For many millions of years, in many worlds.
Only to collide and merge star dust with rock,
Arriving here on Earth by coincidence.
Or just gravity.
To light up all the faces of the moon
Give a purpose to our sun
Once more.
In a new world
Reborn.

MUSE

by Veera Laine,
Teacher from Finland

You are muse
Goddess in disguise
So full full full
Full of beauty
Full of light
Full of words of life

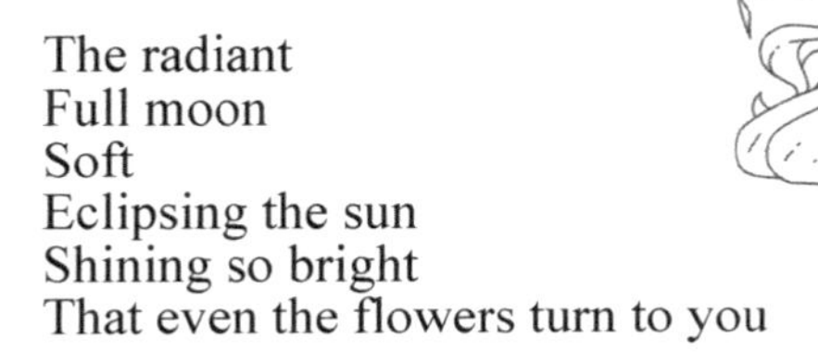

The radiant
Full moon
Soft
Eclipsing the sun
Shining so bright
That even the flowers turn to you

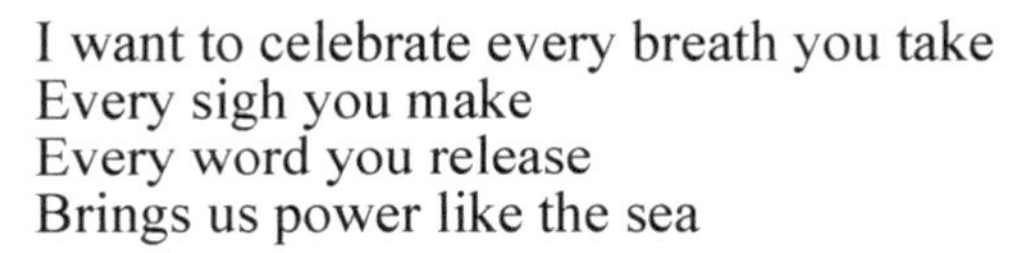

I want to celebrate every breath you take
Every sigh you make
Every word you release
Brings us power like the sea

I go happy
I go bliss
When I know
You created
Birthed this poet
Into existence

Even birds fly to see
Who is this radiant being?
Breathing life
Chanting worlds into existence

Illuminated Heart

by Sylvia Berrevoet,
Transformational Coach and Children's Book Writer,
from The Netherlands and Belgium

Remember that dark clear night
Millions of stars up in the sky
So close we could almost touch them
We felt exhilarated, high
On freedom

It is the night my heart married the moon
And became
The one that could not be broken
The one that shines
From a light within
So pure
One sound
One beat

The intentions born from here
Are heard by one
By many

Connect to that place
You do not have to search
It is there
It was always there
You just misunderstood
So undo the thought
And descend to the centre
Where heart and moon are one
And from there
You will shine
Your love.

Nourished By The Moon

by Cezarina Trone,
Author of The Art of Being a Woman, Yoga Teacher and Modern Mystic, from Romania and Canada

She silently called out to the Moon:

I see you, my Beloved Queen of the Night
Regina Noptii (as they call you in Romania)
You never cease to enchant and illuminate me.
My Muse…my playmate and soul friend.
You were my maid of honor in Tuscany
and you continue to be my Dream Companion,
the vastness of my feeling realm incarnate.
I adore your light.

And the Moon heard it all.
And time stood still.

NAKED MOON

by Ariees Roman,
Author of Nascent Spring and Poetry of Two Worlds

She is the "I am" that gives life…beautiful and divine,
a goddess in human disguise.
And she tells you a story about love
You love her for her reflecting shine,
For the nights of company with soft light.
But here I am, she says.
With no gloss
Do you still love me?
She wants you to see her
With her dark shades,
With the shadows that eclipse her lustre
That keep her from shining.
She finally reveals her true identity—
Takes off the veil.
She wants you to tell her the truth
For now the time has come.
And you see the craters and the gray dust,
Empty spaces
Missing shine she emits at night
The blue soft light, all eclipsed.
She's been your company in her beauty,
Now she waits for you—naked.
Afraid of what you might whisper.
You smile, for you've never seen her
Like this before, her essence laid bare
And you love her evermore.

ACKNOWLEDGEMENTS

There are so many people that have made my life better in so many ways. Either people I have met personally or people I have met through their books, their teachings or their life's journeys. So many personal imprints that together make the fabric of my being and more specifically, its expression through this book.

Starting with my family, our parents teach us everything, whether perceived good or bad - you will either want to be like them, or the opposite of them, which is all the same. And that is everything, the real *neti neti*, the real deal, the rubber hitting the road. Amazing teachers my parents, Dumitra and Vasile. My son Benito, who has been referred to as Jesus or Baby Buddha, with his uncanny clarity and serenity since birth, kept peaking his head though the door throughout the writing of this book to gently push me in the direction of completing it. As well as bringing numerous amounts of drinks and snacks (guided by head chef, his aunty, my sister Mari) to save me going up and down the stairs, which ruins not only the creative flow, but my damaged knees.

My sisters, who would I be without them…just not the same. Sisters are best friends and mothers and fathers and brothers and house keepers and nurses and chefs and stylists and everything in between. Both of my sisters took the brunt of life ahead of me so I can observe and learn quickly, they saved me from so many bumps in the road. My sister Doina taught me how to read when I was five and was the first to read this book and give it the best review I could imagine. And Mari, who has overcome the most adverse situations possible, teaching me and all of us how to be kinder to ourselves (plus cooking and cleaning while I wrote. Seriously, this kind of support is undervalued in the world).

And then there's my teachers lineage. I have utmost respect and gratitude for the work of Byron Katie, the ultimate beacon of unified wisdom on the planet. And so much love for Adyashanti and Mukti, the masters of silent inquiry, the best hosts for silent retreats and best examples of masculine and feminine together that I have ever experienced. Just being in their presence, with no outer conversation, has done more for the spirit than I can express in words.

In writing this book I got to learn about some magnificent women and goddesses and priestesses who paved the road for us to follow. Through a series of coincidences, Enheduanna, the first recorded author and poet in history, an ancient Mesopotamian High Priestess and ruler of the Akkadian and Sumerian people around 4000 years ago, found me. I cannot understand how this legendary woman is not more celebrated. She is the first to take cuneiform (the first form of the alphabet) which was only used for accounting purposes and use it to express herself in a literary poetic form. She is the first to write authored poetry as odes to Innana, the Divine Feminine Goddess and to Nana - Goddess of the Moon.

The first one to refer to as 'I', bringing personal identity and inner consciousness into writing.

She is also the first High Priestess to be exiled. During that time period, no matter what war was taking place, the rule was that the High Priestesses, guarding the connection with heaven, would not be touched or endangered. Well that didn't apply to her, as her enemy feared her powerful leadership and she was locked up. During her exile she wrote the Hymns to Innana and Nana. Somehow as she was writing these prayers to the divine, the army of her father started winning and she was eventually released, then becoming the ruler of the unified city-state of Ur for the rest of her life.

I had already written half the book before I learned all this. It was my sweet friend Veera, who gasped, when hearing a sample of the book for the very first time: "Paula you are channelling Enhedunana". Although I knew Enheduanna was the first known poet in history, I had no idea about her life. Or about the descent and re-emergence of the Divine Feminine energy on Earth mythology and symbolism. That's what friends are for!

The Epilogue was added after the author's copy arrived. It's simply an expression of gratitute towards my friends whom upon reading some of the poems, simply reflected back the energy, care and efforts expressed here. They were all tuned into the same universal longing, at the same time, in different parts of the world.

This brings me to my soul family and my friends at the Poetry club, especially Sylvia and Veera who constantly supported and cheered on me along the way, Pearl and Asmeeta who would join from the other side of the world, in South Africa to just read poetry together.

My coach, Monica for all her patience and her ever so generous ear to anything I had to say or question. Andra for showing up to my first real-life poetry reading with fuchsia roses. All my friends from work (investment banking) who didn't cringe when I told them I was writing poetry, instead showed their support.

Last but not least, I feel I need to acknowledge the dark gurus in my life, those who through their actions shed light onto my own shadows, those who were cruel to be kind and those who were asleep to their own limiting beliefs, so that I can see mine. As they helped me more than anyone, to wake up to my own shadow, to break my heart open so more love can come in and without whom this book would have probably been much more shallow. As BK said to me during one of her amazing calls:
"Don't wake the baby". Let them sleep, may your nights be gentle. I continue to grow the best way I can and this is my only business: who do I become.

I think I have included everyone now and it feels like we have come full circle, or should I say full moon cycle.
Checked to see where the moon was during my writing, just for fun. I have started writing the book on a full moon night and I have completed all the poems written here, on 4th of November 2021, a New Moon night. As I am closing here today on 5th of November 2021, after 11 months, the moon is Waxing Crescent 1%. That is when the light is only a slighter on the edge to the right of the moon. When new light from the sun makes its way to the face of the moon, to fill it up once again, to light our nights and our hearts.

With Love and Devotion,

Your Priestess.

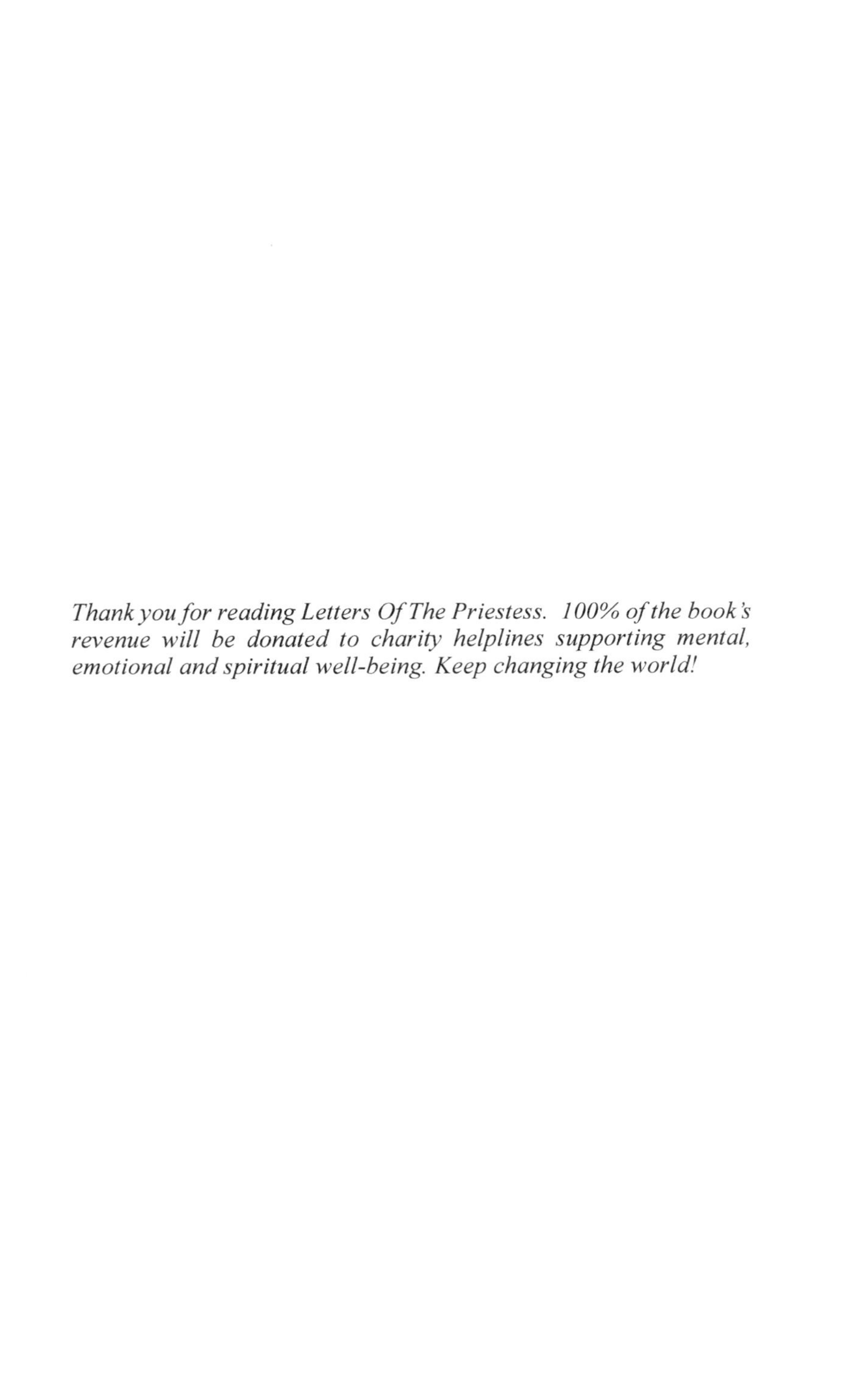

Thank you for reading Letters Of The Priestess. 100% of the book's revenue will be donated to charity helplines supporting mental, emotional and spiritual well-being. Keep changing the world!

AUTHOR'S PAGE:

www.paulacurteanu.com

AUTHOR'S PODCAST: POETRY DRIP

Available on Spotify, Apple Podcasts and anywhere you enjoy your podcasts

SOCIAL MEDIA

Instagram: @paulacurteanu

OTHER RESOURCES

Byron Katie - The Work: www.thework.com

Adya and Mukti's Open Gate Sangha:
https://www.opengatesangha.org

Inanna, The Lady Of The Largest Heart by Enheduanna

This book was edited and put together in November 2021, when we also witnessed the longest Red Moon eclipse in 600 years. All in all, a memorable year.

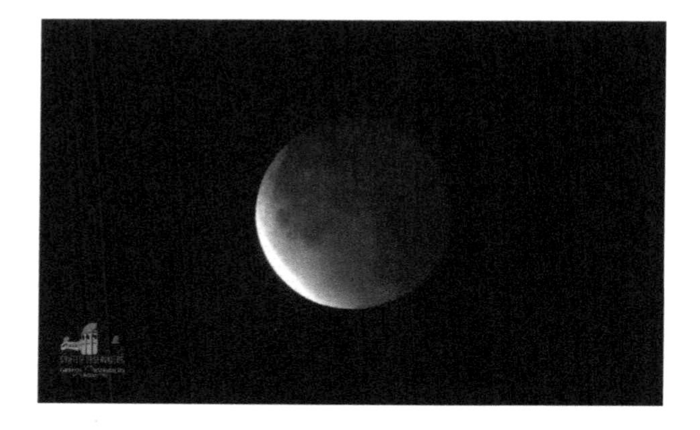

Photo is a screenhot taken by Paula watching the eclipse online, kindly broadcasted by Griffith Observatory in California.

Thank you for reading and remember to walk with your head held high and sometimes even look up at the sky. We are all made from stars and moons. x

CPSIA information can be obtained
at www.ICGtesting.com
Printed in the USA
LVHW072205310122
709869LV00011B/488